The History of Eucharistic Adoration:
Development of Doctrine in the Catholic Church

By John A. Hardon, S.J.

In an age of widespread confusion and disbelief, this document offers unprecedented clarity in the most important element of our faith. I recommend that it be prayerfully studied and widely circulated. It is thoroughly researched and well documented, and promises to enlighten, instruct and inspire countless souls to an undying love of our Eucharistic Lord.

Bishop Jerome J. Hastrich,
Former Bishop of Gallup, New Mexico, U.S.A.

Contents

Introduction

The phenomenal growth of devotion to the Real Presence of Christ in the Holy Eucharist has puzzled not a few sincere people. Nocturnal Adoration societies, Perpetual Adoration groups, national associations of the faithful promoting organized visits to the Blessed Sacrament, Holy Hours before the tabernacle, monthly, weekly and even daily exposition of the Eucharist in churches and chapels, in one country after another, have become commonplace.

What to make of all of this? Is this another form of pious eccentricity, or is it founded on authentic Catholic doctrine and grounded on the solid rock of Christian revelation?

It is authentic Catholic doctrine and it rests on the unchangeable truth of our revealed faith. But it needs to be explained, and the explanation is a classic example of what we call *development of doctrine.*

By development of doctrine, we mean that some divinely revealed truth has become more deeply understood and more clearly perceived than it had been before. Under the guidance of the Holy Spirit, whom Christ promised to send to teach us, the Church comes to see more deeply what she had always believed, and the resulting insights find expression in devotion of the faithful that may have been quite uncommon in the Church's previous history. The whole spectrum of Christology and Mariology has witnessed such dogmatic progress. Adoration of the Eucharist, therefore, is simply another, though dramatic, example of doctrinal development.

Always implied in such progress is that, objectively, the revealed truth remains constant and unchanged. But through the light of the Holy Spirit, the subjective understanding of the truth becomes more clear, its meaning becomes more certain and its grasp by the believing mind becomes increasingly more firm.

Our purpose in this short study is to show how the Real Presence of Christ in the Eucharist has undergone a marvelous development over the centuries. We are now witnessing what can only be described as the work of the Holy Spirit, whom Christ promised, "the Father will send in my name. He will teach you all things, and bring to your mind whatever I have said to you" (John 14:25).

Apostolic Times to the Early Middle Ages

Belief in the real, physical presence of Christ in the Eucharist grew out of the teaching of the evangelists and St. Paul. They made it plain to the apostolic Church that the Eucharistic elements were literally Jesus Christ continuing His saving mission among men.

John and Paul were especially plain. The skepticism of Christ's followers, when He preached the reality of His Body and Blood as food and drink, made John record the fact that "many of His disciples withdrew and no longer went about with Him." Seeing this, Jesus asked the twelve, "Do you also want to leave me?" Simon Peter did not understand any more than those who left Christ, but his loyalty was more firm. "Lord," he answered, "to whom shall we go" (John 6:66-68) ?

Paul's letter to the Corinthians rebuked them for making the Agape, which should have been a beautiful sign of unity, into an occasion of discord. He reminded them that the Eucharist is no ordinary food. It is actually the Body and Blood of Christ according to "the tradition which I handed on to you that came to me from the Lord Himself" (1 Corinthians 11: 23-26).

At the turn of the first century, Ignatius of Antioch, on his way to martyrdom in Rome, had to warn the Christians not to be taken in by the Gnostic-a good modern term would be "visionaries," who denied the Real Presence. Ignatius said these people abstained from the Eucharist because they did not accept what true Christians believe, that in the Eucharist is the same Jesus Christ who lived and died and rose from the dead for our salvation.

Under the impact of this faith, the early hermits reserved the Eucharist in their cells. From at least the middle of the third century, it was very general for the solitaries in the East, especially in Palestine and Egypt, to preserve the consecrated elements in the caves or hermitages where they lived.

The immediate purpose of this reservation was to enable the hermits to give themselves Holy Communion. But these hermits were too conscious of what the Real Presence was, not to treat it with great reverence and not to think of it as serving a sacred purpose by just being nearby.

Not only did they have the Sacrament with them in their cells, but they carried it on their persons when they moved from one place to another. This practice was sanctioned by the custom of the *fermentum,* that certainly goes back to as early as 120 A.D. The rite of *fermentum* was a particle of the Eucharist (sometimes dipped in the chalice) transported from the bishop of one diocese to the bishop of another diocese. The latter would then consume the species at his next solemn Mass as a token of unity between the churches. It was called a *fermentum* not necessarily because leavened bread was used but because the Eucharist symbolized the leaven of unity which permeates and transforms Christians, so that they become one with Christ.

Already in the second century, popes sent the Eucharist to other bishops as a pledge of unity of faith; and, on occasion, bishops would do the same for their priests.

As monasticism changed from solitary to community life, the monks received something of the same privilege of carrying the Eucharist with them. They would have it on their persons when working in the fields or going on a voyage. The species was either placed in a small receptacle (chrismal) worn bandoleer-fashion, or in a little bag (perula) hung around the neck under their clothes. Irish and British manuscripts make frequent mention of the practice. It was not only to have the hosts ready for Communion but also to insure safety against robbers and protection against the hazards of travel.

The life of St. Comgall (died 601) tells how on one occasion he was attacked by heathen Pietists while working in a field. On seeing the chrismal around his neck, the attackers did not dare touch him for fear of some retaliation since they surmised (as the narrator says) that Comgall was carrying his God. The saint was so moved by the experience that he exclaimed, "Lord, you are my strength, my refuge, and my Redeemer."

As early as the Council of Nicea (325) we know that the Eucharist began to be reserved in the churches of monasteries and convents. Again, the immediate reason for this reservation was for the sick and the dying, and also for the ceremony of the *fermentum*. But naturally its sacred character was recognized and the place of reservation was set off from profane usage.

From the beginning of community life, therefore, the Blessed Sacrament became an integral part of the church structure of a monastery. A bewildering variety of names was used to identify the place of reservation. *Pastoforium, diakonikon, secretarium, prothesis* are the most common. As far as we can tell, the Eucharist was originally kept in a special room, just off the sanctuary but separated from the church where Mass was offered.

Certainly by the 800's, the Blessed Sacrament was kept within the monastic church itself, close to the altar. In fact, we have a poem from the year 802, telling of a pyx containing the Sacred Species reserved on the high altar of the abbey church at Lindisfarne in England.

The practice of reserving the Eucharist in religious houses was so universal that there is no evidence to the contrary even before the year 1000. In fact, numerous regulations are extant which provided for protection of the sacred elements, as the wording went, "from profanation by mice and impious men." The species were to be kept under lock and key and sometimes in a receptacle raised high enough to be out of easy reach of profaning hands.

It is interesting to note that one of the first unmistakable references to reserving the Blessed Sacrament is found in a life of St. Basil (who died in 379). Basil is said to have divided the Eucharistic Bread into three parts when he celebrated Mass in the monastery. One part he consumed, the second part he gave to the monks, and the third he placed in a golden dove suspended over the altar.

This would suggest that, though we have less access to Oriental sources, the Eastern monasteries were centuries ahead of the West in reserving the Eucharistic elements in the monastic church proper and not only in a separate place.

Among the treasures of Monte Cassino that seem to have been destroyed during the Second World War were two small ancient tabernacles, one of gold and the other of silver. They were gifts of Pope Victor III (died 1087), who had been abbot at Cassino before his election to the papacy.

Berengarius to
St. Francis of Assisi

Toward the end of the eleventh century we enter on a new era in the history of Eucharistic adoration. Until then the Real Presence was taken for granted in Catholic belief and its reservation was the common practice in Catholic churches, including the chapels and oratories of religious communities. Suddenly a revolution hit the Church when Berengarius (999-1088), archdeacon of Angers in France, publicly denied that Christ was really and physically present under the species of bread and wine. Others took up the idea and began writing about the Eucharistic Christ as not exactly the Christ of the Gospels or, by implication, as not actually there.

The matter became so serious that Pope Gregory VII ordered Berengarius to sign a retraction. This credo has made theological history. It was the Church's first definitive statement of what had always been believed and never seriously challenged. The witness came from the abbot-become-pope, whose faith in the Blessed Sacrament had been nourished for years in a Benedictine monastery.

Gregory's teaching on the Real Presence was quoted verbatim in Pope Paul VI's historic document *Mysterium Fidei* (1965) to meet a new challenge to the Eucharist in our day — very similar to what happened in the eleventh century.

I believe in my heart and openly profess that the bread and wine placed upon the altar are, by the mystery of the sacred prayer and the words of the Redeemer, substantially changed into the true and life-giving flesh and blood of Jesus Christ our Lord, and that after the consecration, there is present the true body of Christ which was born of the Virgin and offered up for the salvation of the world, hung on the cross and now sits at the right hand of the Father, and that there is present the true blood of Christ which flowed from His side. They are present not only by means of a sign and of the efficacy of the Sacrament, but also in the very reality and truth of their nature and substance.

With this profession of faith, the churches of Europe began what can only be described as a Eucharistic Renaissance. Processions of the Blessed Sacrament were instituted; prescribed acts of adoration were legislated; visits to Christ in the pyx were encouraged; the cells of anchoresses had windows made into the church to allow the religious to view and adore before the tabernacle. An early ordinal of the Carmelites included the words "for the devotion of those in the choir" when referring to the reservation of the species.

From the eleventh century on, devotion to the Blessed Sacrament reserved in the tabernacle became more and more prevalent in the Catholic world. At every stage in this development, members of religious orders of men and women took the lead.

The Benedictine Lanfranc, as Archbishop of Canterbury, introduced from France into England numerous customs affecting the worship of the Real Presence.

St. Francis of Assisi, who was never ordained a priest, had a great personal devotion to Christ in the Blessed Sacrament. His first admonition on the Holy Eucharist could not have been more precise.

Sacred Scripture tells us that the Father dwells in "light inaccessible" (1 Timothy 6:16) and that "God is spirit" (John 4:24) and St. John adds, "No one at any time has seen God" (John 1:18). Because God is a spirit He can be seen only in spirit; "It is the spirit that gives life; the flesh profits nothing " (John 6:63). But God the Son is equal to the Father and so He too can be seen only in the same way as the Father and the Holy Spirit. That is why all those were condemned who saw our Lord Jesus Christ in His humanity but did not see or believe in spirit in His divinity, that He was the true Son of God. In the same way now, all those are damned who see the Sacrament of the Body of Christ which is consecrated on the altar in the form of bread and wine by the words of our Lord in the hands of the priest, and do not see or believe in spirit and in God that this is really the most holy Body and Blood of our Lord Jesus Christ.

It was this clear faith in Christ's presence in the Eucharist that sustained Francis during his severest trials. It was this same faith which inspired a whole new tradition among religious communities of women. Convents had the Sacrament reserved for adoration apart from Mass and Holy Communion.

Feast of Corpus Christi. There was nothing startling, therefore, when Pope Urban IV, in the thirteenth century, instituted the feast of Corpus Christi. When establishing this feast, the Pope stressed the love of Christ who wished to remain physically with us until the end of time.

In the Eucharist, said the Pope, "Christ is with us in His own substance." For "when telling the Apostles that He was ascending into heaven, He said, 'Behold I am with you all days, even to the consummation of the world,' thus comforting them with the gracious promise that He would remain and be with them even by His bodily presence" (August 11, 1264).

Urban IV commissioned Thomas Aquinas to compose the Liturgy of the Hours for the feast of Corpus Christi, to be celebrated annually on the Thursday following Trinity Sunday.

Three hymns which Aquinas composed for the feast are among the most beautiful in the Catholic liturgy. They express the unchangeable faith of the Church in the abiding Presence of her Founder on earth. They also explain why the faithful adore Christ in the Blessed Sacrament. All three hymns are part of the Divine Office. They are best known by each of their last two verses, which have become part of the treasury of Catholic hymnology.

- *O Salutaris Hostia* is an act of adoration of Christ the Saving Victim who opened wide the gate of heaven to man below.

- *Tantum Ergo Sacramentum* is an act of adoration of the Word-made-flesh, where faith supplies for what the senses cannot perceive.

- *Panis Angelicus* is an act of adoration of that Wondrous Thing where the lowly and poor are fed, banqueting on their Incarnate Lord and King.

Aquinas, like the Church, never separated the Eucharist as Sacrifice, Communion and Presence. But, with the Church, he also realized that without the Real Presence there would be no real sacrifice nor real communion. Aquinas assumed that God became man so He might offer Himself on Calvary and continue to offer Himself in the Mass. He became man that He might give Himself to the disciples at the Last Supper and continue to give Himself to us in Holy Communion. He became man to live in flesh and blood in Palestine and continue to live now on earth as the same Jesus who died and rose from the dead and is seated at the right hand of His heavenly Father.

Middle Ages to the Council of Trent

Since Pope Urban IV instituted the feast of Corpus Christi, the bishops of Rome had been vigilant to protect the Church's faith in her Founder's unceasing presence on earth in the Holy Eucharist. But every time a new difficulty arose, it became a stimulus to making this faith more clear and meaningful, in a word there was increased development of Eucharistic doctrine.

Before the Council of Trent. A variety of situations occasioned papal declarations of the Eucharist.

In the fourteenth century, the Armenians asked Clement VI for financial assistance to pay the heavy subsidies laid on them by the reigning sultan. Correspondence with the Armenian bishops made him wonder if they professed the full Catholic faith. Among other propositions he required them to accept was the statement that, "After the words of consecration there is present numerically the same *(idem numero)* Body of Christ as was born of the Virgin and was immolated on the Cross" (September 29, 1351).

Twenty years later, a theoretical question was raised that had serious practical implications. Some writers speculated whether Christ still remained in the Eucharist when the sacred species were desecrated. Pope Gregory XI demanded rejection of the following statements:

If a consecrated Host falls or is thrown into a sewer, the mud, or some other profane place, even though the species remain, the Body of Christ ceases to be present and the substance of bread returns.

If a consecrated Host is eaten or consumed by a rodent or some other animal, even while the species remain, the Body of Christ ceases to be present under the species and the substance of bread returns (August 8, 1371).

More serious was the problem created by the so-called Calixtines in the fifteenth century. They claimed that the whole Christ is not received unless the faithful receive Holy Communion under both forms, including the chalice. This time, the General Council of Constance decided to "declare, decree and define" as an article of faith that "the entire Body and Blood of Christ are truly contained both under the species of bread and under the species of wine." This definition was confirmed by Pope Martin V (September 1, 1425). The implications for the exposition and adoration of the Eucharist are obvious.

The Council of Trent. By the sixteenth century, the whole spectrum of Catholic belief in the Holy Eucharist was challenged by the Reformers. As a consequence, the Council of Trent treated this subject exhaustively. Every aspect of the Sacrifice of the Mass, Holy Communion and the Real Presence was clarified and defined.

For our purpose, the Council's teaching on the Real Presence was historic. It was the dawn of the most significant development of Eucharistic doctrine since apostolic times. Even a few sentences from Trent are revealing.

> *The other sacraments do not have the power of sanctifying until someone makes use of them, but in the Eucharist the very Author of sanctity is present before the Sacrament is used. For before the apostles received the Eucharist from the hands of our Lord, He told them that it was His Body that He was giving them.*
>
> *The Church of God has always believed that immediately after the consecration the true Body and Blood of our Lord, together with His soul and divinity, exists under the species of bread and wine. His Body exists under the species of bread and His Blood under the species of wine according to the import of the words. But His Body exists under the species of wine, His Blood under the species of bread, and His soul under both species in virtue of the natural connection and concomitance which unite the parts of Christ our Lord, who has risen from the dead and dies now no more.*

Moreover, Christ's divinity is present because of its admirable hypostatic union with His body and soul. It is, therefore, perfectly true that just as much is present under either species as is present under both. For Christ, whole and entire, exists under the species of bread and under any part of that species, and similarly the whole Christ exists under the species of wine and under its parts.

Given this fact of faith, Trent could logically go on to declare that,

"The only-begotten Son of God is to be adored in the Holy Sacrament of the Eucharist with the worship of latria, including external worship. The Sacrament, therefore, is to be honored with extraordinary festive celebrations (and) solemnly carried from place to place in processions according to the praiseworthy universal rite and custom of the holy Church. The Sacrament is to be publicly exposed for the people's adoration."

Approved by Pope Julius III (October 11, 1551), these conciliar statements became the foundation for dogmatic and devotional progress ever since.

Development of Eucharistic Adoration

As we have seen, there had been reservation and adoration of the Blessed Sacrament since the early days of the Church. But with the Council of Trent began a new era in the devotion of the faithful to Christ's Real Presence in the Eucharist.

The Forty-Hours Devotion. Before the end of the sixteenth century, Pope Clement VIII in 1592 issued a historic document on what was called in Italian *Quarant' Ore* (Forty Hours).

The devotion consisted of forty hours of continual prayer before the Blessed Sacrament exposed. Introduced earlier on a local scale in Milan, the Bishop of Rome not only authorized the devotion for Rome, but explained how it should be practiced.

> *We have determined to establish publicly in this Mother City of Rome an uninterrupted course of prayer in such ways that in the different churches [he specifies them] on appointed days, there be observed the pious and salutary devotion of the Forty Hours; with such an arrangement of churches and times that, at every hour of the day and night, the incense of prayer shall ascend without intermission before the face of the Lord.*

About a century later (1731) his successor, Clement XIII, published a detailed set of instructions for the proper carrying out of the Forty-Hours devotion, for example:

- The Blessed Sacrament is always exposed on the high altar, except in patriarchal basilicas.

- Statues, relics and pictures around the altar of exposition are to be removed or veiled.

- Only clerics in surplices may take care of the altar of exposition.

- There must be continuous relays of worshipers before the Blessed Sacrament and should include a priest or cleric in major orders.

- No Masses are to be said at the altar of exposition.

Gradually the Forty Hours devotion spread throughout the Catholic world. Proposed by the Code of Canon Law in 1917, the new Code states that in churches or oratories where the Eucharist is reserved:

> *It is recommended (commendatur) . . . that there be held each year a solemn exposition of the Blessed Sacrament for an appropriate, even if not for a continuous, time so that the local community may more attentively meditate on and adore the Eucharistic Mystery (Canon 942).*

Perpetual Adoration. The term "perpetual adoration" is broadly used to designate the practically uninterrupted adoration of the Blessed Sacrament. The term may mean several things:

- The adoration is literally perpetual, so that someone is always in prayer before the Holy Eucharist.

- The adoration is morally perpetual, with only such short interruptions as imperative reasons or uncontrollable circumstances require.

- The adoration is uninterrupted for a longer or shorter period, a day or several days, as in the Forty-Hours devotion.

- The adoration is uninterrupted in one special church or chapel.

- The adoration is uninterrupted in different churches or chapels in a locality like a diocese or a country, or throughout the world.

Some writers trace the first beginnings of perpetual adoration to the late fourth century, when converts to the faith in some dioceses were to adore the Blessed Sacrament exposed for eight days after their baptism. It is certain, however, that even before the institution of the feast of Corpus Christi, not only religious in convents and monasteries but the laity practiced Eucharistic adoration.

After his victory over the Albigenses, King Louis VII of France asked the Bishop of Avignon to have the Blessed Sacrament exposed in the Chapel of the Holy Cross (September 14, 1226). The throng of adorers was so great that the bishop decided to have the adoration continue day and night. This was later ratified by the Holy See and continued uninterrupted until 1792 during the French Revolution. It was resumed in 1829.

It was not until after the Council of Trent, however, that perpetual adoration began to develop on a worldwide scale. We may distinguish especially the following forms.

Cloistered Religious Institutes were founded for the express purpose of adoring the Holy Eucharist day and night. Some, like the Benedictines of the Perpetual Adoration of the Blessed Sacrament in Austria (1654), took a solemn vow of perpetual adoration.

Apostolic Religious Institutes were started to both practice adoration themselves and promote perpetual worship of the Eucharist among the faithful. Thus began the Congregation of the Sacred Hearts of Jesus and Mary, and of the Perpetual Adoration of the Blessed Sacrament of the Altar. Formally approved in 1817, its aim is to honor and imitate the four states of Christ's life to be honored and imitated by the exercise of adoration of the Eucharist.

Men's Nocturnal Adoration societies began on an international scale in Rome in 1810 with the founding of the Pious Union of the Adorers of the Most Blessed Sacrament. They spread throughout Europe and into North and South America. Their focus was (and is) on perpetual adoration in the strict sense.

Perpetual Eucharistic Associations of the faithful go back to the seventeenth century. One of the earliest was started by Baron de Renty in 1641 at St. Paul's parish in Paris. It was a perpetual adoration society for ladies. At Boulonge in France (1753), the parishes were divided into twelve groups representing the twelve months of the year. Each group contained as many parishes as there were days in the month it represented. Each church in every group was assigned one day for Eucharistic adoration.

Among the apostles of perpetual adoration for the laity, none has had a more lasting influence in the modern world than St. Peter Julian Eymard. In 1856 he founded the Blessed Sacrament Fathers in Paris and two years later, with Marguerite Guillot, he established the Servants of the Blessed Sacrament, a cloistered contemplative congregation of women. Peter Eymard's published conferences on the Real Presence have inspired numerous lay associations. They have taken his words literally when he said,

In the presence of Jesus Christ in the Most Blessed Sacrament, all greatness disappears, all holiness humbles itself and comes to nothing. Jesus Christ is there!

Visits to the Blessed Sacrament. Not unlike perpetual adoration, so the history of visits to the Blessed Sacrament is best known from the monastic spirituality of the early Middle Ages. In the thirteenth century Ancren Riwle, or Rule for Anchoresses, the nuns were to begin their day by a visit to the Blessed Sacrament.

Priests also, who had easy access to the reserved Holy Eucharist, would regularly visit Our Lord in the Blessed Sacrament. Thus the martyr, St. Thomas a Becket (1118-1170), in one of his letters writes to a friend,

If you do not harken to me who have been wont to pray for you in an abundance of tears and with groanings not a few before the Majesty of the Body of Christ (Materials, V, 276).

By the fourteenth century, we read how the English mystic, Richard Rolle, strongly exhorts Christians to visit the nearby church as often as they can. Why? Because:

In the church is most devotion to pray, for there is God upon the altar to hear those who pray to Him and to grant them what they ask and what is best for them (Works, I, 145).

Church historians tell us that by the end of the century, the practice of people visiting the Blessed Sacrament became fairly common.

One of the sobering facts of the Reformation is to know what happened when the English Reformers separated from Rome. At first they did not forbid the clergy to reserve some of both species after the Lord's Supper ceremony — to be taken to the sick and the dying. But before long, reservation of the Eucharistic elements became rare. This was to be expected after the Thirty Nine Articles (1571) declared that transubstantiation was untrue and that the Eucharist should not be worshipped or carried about in procession.

Three hundred years later, the Anglicans, who started the Oxford Movement, restored continuous reservation of the Eucharist and encouraged visits to the Blessed Sacrament. Credit for this return to Catholic Eucharistic piety belongs to the Anglican Sisterhood of St. Margaret, founded in 1854. The community records show that soon after its foundation the sisters were making daily visits to the Eucharist in their oratory and, about the same time, Benediction of the Blessed Sacrament was introduced.

In the Catholic Church, visits to the Blessed Sacrament have become a standard part of personal and communal prayer. The first Code of Canon Law urged the "faithful to visit the Most Blessed Sacrament as often as possible" (Canon 1273). The new Code is more specific.

> *Unless there is a grave reason to the contrary, a church, in which the Blessed Eucharist is reserved, is to be open to the faithful for at least some hours every day, so that they can pray before the Blessed Sacrament (Canon 937).*

Members of religious institutes are simply told that each day they are to "adore the Lord Himself present in the Sacrament" (Canon 663, #2).

Benediction of the Blessed Sacrament. As with other Eucharistic devotions, Benediction, as it is commonly called, began in the thirteenth century. It was strongly influenced by the establishment of the feast of Corpus Christi. Two hymns, especially *O Salutaris Hostia* and *Tantum Ergo*, composed by St. Thomas Aquinas, became part of the Benediction service.

One aspect of the history of Benediction that is not commonly known is its early association with devotion to the Blessed Virgin. This was already expressed in the *Pange Lingua* for the First Vespers of the Corpus Christi liturgy, saying, "To us He was given, to us He was born of a pure Virgin." Except for Mary, there would have been no Incarnation, and except for the Incarnation, there would be no Eucharist.

As related by historians, by the early thirteenth century there were organized confraternities and guilds in great numbers, whose custom was to sing canticles in the evening of the day before a statue of Our Lady. The canticles were called *Laudes* (praises) and were often composed in the vernacular or even the local dialect of the people. In the hands of people such as the Franciscan Giacopone da Todi (1230-1306), these hymns helped to develop a native Italian literature. The confraternities were called *Laudesi*.

With the stimulus given by the Feast of Corpus Christi, these Marian canticle meetings were often accompanied by exposition of the Blessed Sacrament. What began as a practice to add solemnity to the Marian devotions became, in time, a distinctive form of Eucharistic piety.

In France these Marian canticle sessions were called *Salut*, in the Low Countries *Lof*, in Germany and England simply *Salve*.

They were gradually combined with exposition of the Eucharist, especially when the Blessed Sacrament was carried in procession and/or the sick were blessed with the Holy Eucharist. When people made out their wills, many included bequests for the continucd support of these evening song-fests honoring Our Lady and would specify that the Blessed Sacrament should be exposed during the whole time of the *Salut*. The generations-old practice of blessing the sick with the Holy Eucharist at Lourdes is merely an extension of this combining of Benediction with devotion to the Blessed Virgin Mary.

Eucharistic Congresses. As public demonstrations of faith in the Real Presence, local Eucharistic congresses go back to the Middle Ages. But the first international congress grew out of the zeal of Marie-Marthe Tamisier (1834-1910), a French laywoman who from childhood had an extraordinary devotion to the Blessed Sacrament. She called a day without Holy Communion her Good Friday. Having several times tried unsuccessfully to enter a religious community, she spent much of her life spreading devotion to the Real Presence. Inspired by the conferences of Peter Julian Eymard and directed by Abbot Chevier of Lyons, she first promoted pilgrimages to shrines where Eucharistic miracles were reported to have taken place. Finally the first international Eucharistic Congress was held at Lille in 1881. At the fifth Congress at Toulouse in 1886, over fifteen hundred bishops and priests, and thirty thousand of the laity participated.

By now international congresses have been held on all the continents, including Africa, Asia and Australia. Pope Paul VI attended the thirty-eighth and thirty-ninth Eucharistic congresses at Bombay in 1964 and Bogota in 1968. Pope John Paul II was to have attended the centenary congress at Lourdes in 1981, but was prevented because of the assassination attempt on his life on May 13th of that year.

National congresses have become widespread. During one of these, at Bogota in 1980, Pope John Paul II synthesized the role which, in God's providence, a Eucharistic congress is meant to serve.

The Eucharistic Congress is first and foremost a great community act of faith in the presence and in the action of Jesus in the Eucharist, who remains with us sacramentally to travel with us along our ways, so that with His power, we can cope with our problems, our toil, our suffering.

From this moment let us unite round the consecrated Host, the divine Pilgrim among pilgrims, eager to draw from Him the inspiration and strength to make ours the needs and aspirations of our emigrant brothers.

The Eucharistic Congress should demonstrate particularly and highlight the fact that the People of God here on earth lives by the Eucharist, that it draws from It its strength for everyday toils and for the struggles in all spheres of its existence (June 30 and July 9, 1980).

More than a century of experience has verified this judgment of the Pope.

Why Development of Eucharistic Doctrine

We now move from considering development of Eucharistic adoration to progress in Eucharistic doctrine. The two forms of development are related, but they are not the same.

We may say that, historically, the growth in devotion led to development of doctrine. But saying this is not yet proving it. And our purpose from here on will be to show how the blessings experienced by the faithful from their worship of the Blessed Sacrament led, under the Church's guidance, to a phenomenal growth in understanding the Real Presence as a marvelous source of grace to those who believe.

Basic Premises of Doctrinal Development. The Second Vatican Council will go down in history as the Council of dogmatic progress. It was exactly four hundred years since the close of the Council of Trent (1563), when the Second Vatican Council opened (1962).

During these four centuries, one after another of the cardinal mysteries of the Christian faith had grown immensely. The essential deposit of faith has remained the same, of course. But the meaning of this faith had developed to a degree that has scandalized many, been misunderstood by others and, we may say, is recognized by relatively few.

It is not surprising, therefore, that Vatican II should have laid down the basic principles for dogmatic development. After declaring that divine revelation, found in Sacred Scripture and Tradition, has been entrusted for safe-keeping by the Church, the Council goes on to say that there is more to the Church's role than just preserving revealed truth. Her mission is also to provide for growth in assimilating this truth. The revealed deposit "that comes from the apostles makes progress in the Church, with the help of the Holy Spirit."

> *There is a growth in insight into the realities and words that are passed on. This comes about in various ways. It comes through the contemplation and study of believers who ponder these things in their hearts. It comes from the intimate sense of spiritual realities which they experience. And it comes from the preaching of those who received, along with their rights of succession in the episcopate, the sure charism of truth. Thus, as the centuries go by, the Church is always advancing towards the plenitude of divine truth, until eventually the words of God are fulfilled in her (Dogmatic Constitution on Divine Revelation, II, 8).*

Among the ways that the Church has grown in her understanding of the Sacrament of the Eucharist, we shall concentrate on only one, namely "experience."

Experienced Benefits of Eucharistic Adoration. The Council of Trent declared that Christ should be worshipped now in the Eucharist no less than He had been in first century Palestine. Why? Because in the Blessed Sacrament "it is the same God whom the apostles adored in Galilee" (Decree on the Holy Eucharist, chapter 5). The adorableness of the Eucharistic Christ, therefore, is an article of the Catholic faith.

What has become increasingly clear, however, is that Christ in the Eucharist is not only adorable but entreatable. He is not only to be adored, like Thomas did, by addressing Him as, "My Lord and my God." He is also to be asked for what we need, like the blind man who begged, "Lord, that I may see," or approached like the woman who said to herself, "If I can even touch His clothes, I shall be well again." By now countless believers have begged the Savior in the Eucharist for what they needed, and have come close to Him in the tabernacle or on the altar. Their resulting experience has profoundly deepened the Church's realization of how literally Christ spoke when He promised to be with us until the end of time.

The experience has been mainly spiritual: In giving light to the mind and strength to the will, in providing graces for oneself and others, in enabling weak human nature to suffer superhuman trials, in giving ordinary people supernatural power to accomplish extraordinary deeds.

Sts. John Fisher (1469-1535) and Thomas More (1478-1535) were strengthened in life and prepared themselves for martyrdom by fervent adoration of the Blessed Sacrament. In one of More's prayers, published after his death, we read,

> *O sweet Savior Christ, by the divers torments of Thy most bitter Passion, take from me, good Lord, this lukewarm fashion or rather key-cold meditation, and this dullness in praying to Thee. And give me Thy grace to long for Thy Holy Sacraments, and especially to rejoice in the Presence of Thy blessed Body, sweet Savior Christ, in the Holy Sacrament of the Altar, and duly to thank Thee for Thy gracious visitation therewith.*

St. Francis Xavier (1506-1552) after preaching and baptizing all day would often spend the night in prayer before the Blessed Sacrament.

St. Mary Magdalen dei Pazzi (1566-1607) was a Carmelite nun from the age of seventeen. She recommended to busy people in the world to take time out each day for praying before the Holy Eucharist. She wrote:

> *A friend will visit a friend in the morning to wish him a good day, in the evening, a good night, taking also an opportunity to converse with him during the day. In like manner, make visits to Jesus Christ in the Blessed Sacrament, if your duties permit it. It is especially at the foot of the altar that one prays well. In all your visits to our Savior, frequently offer His precious Blood to the Eternal Father. You will find these visits very conducive to increase in you divine love.*

St. Margaret Mary (1647-1680), a Visitation nun, found before the Blessed Sacrament the strength she needed to endure what witnesses at her beatification process declared were:

> *contempt, contradictions, rebukes, insults, reproaches, without complaining, and praying for those by whom she was ill-treated.*

St. Alphonsus Liguori (1696-1787), patron saint of confessors, wrote a whole book on visits to the Blessed Sacrament. He advised,

> *withdraw yourself from people and spend at least a quarter of an hour, or a half-hour, in some church in the presence of the Blessed Sacrament. Taste and see how sweet is the Lord, and you will learn from your own experience how many graces this will bring you.*

St. John Vianney, the Curé of Ars (1786-1859), told his people,

> *Our Lord is hidden there in the tabernacle, waiting for us to come and visit Him, and make our requests to Him . . . In heaven, where we shall be glorious and triumphant, we shall see Him in all His glory. If He had presented Himself, before us in that glory now, we should not have dared to approach Him; but He hides Himself like a person in prison, who might say to us, 'You do not see me, but that is no matter. Ask of me all you wish and I will grant it.' The Curé of Ars spent most of his long hours in prayer before the Blessed Sacrament. During his homilies, he would often turn towards the tabernacle, saying with emotion, "He is there!"*

So the litany of witnesses to the power of the Real Presence went on. By the time of the first international Eucharistic Congress in 1881, the evidence was more than sufficient for the Church's magisterium to speak extensively on the subject.

The Church's Magisterium

It was no coincidence that international Eucharistic Congresses came into existence because of the experience of the faithful. As mentioned before, it was a laywoman, Marie-Marthe Tamisier, whose personal awareness of the spiritual energy available from the Real Presence that Providence used to bring about the first international Eucharistic Congress at Lille, in France, in 1881.

In the papal brief which Leo XIII addressed to those attending that Congress, he spoke of the "great joy" he had in commending the bishops who organized the assembly. He approved its purpose, namely "of repairing the iniquities wreaked upon the Most Holy Sacrament and of promoting Its worship." He praised the laymen for "the great extension of the work of Nocturnal Adoration" and for the report of "how this salutary institution is taking root, progressing and bearing fruit everywhere."

The key factor, according to Pope Leo, is that Eucharistic Adoration is bearing supernatural fruit wherever the practice is nourished by the faith of the people.

St. Pius X's devotion to the Real Presence, biographers say, was at the heart of his historic promotion of early and frequent Holy Communion. On the day of his canonization, Pope Pius XII identified the source of his predecessor's apostolic genius:

In the profound vision which he had of the Church as a society, Pope Pius X recognized that it was the Blessed Sacrament which had the power to nourish her intimate life substantially, and to elevate her high above all other human societies (Quest' ora difulgente, May 29, 1954).

Anticipating the publication of his decree on frequent, even daily, Communion (December 20, 1905), Pius X requested that the International Eucharistic Congress that year should be held in Rome. It was the sixteenth in sequence and the first one in the Eternal City. The Pope opened the Congress with the Mass which he celebrated and then participated in the procession with the Blessed Sacrament.

Popes Benedict XV and Pius XI carried on the papal tradition of encouraging adoration of the Holy Eucharist, and prayers of expiation and petition to Our Lord in the Blessed Sacrament.

It was Benedict XV who issued the first Code of Canon Law in 1917 which legislated the reservation of the Blessed Sacrament in "every parish or quasi-parish church, and in the church connected with the residence of exempt men and women religious" (Canon 1265, #1). It was this same Code which encouraged the private and public exposition of the Holy Eucharist.

Pope Pius XI associated the worship of Christ in the Blessed Sacrament with expiation for sin. St. Margaret Mary had been canonized in 1920, just two years before Achille Ratti was elected Pope. In 1928, he wrote a lengthy encyclical on Reparation to the Sacred Heart. Its whole theme is on the desperate need to plead for God's mercy, especially through the Holy Eucharist. During her prayers before the Blessed Sacrament, Christ revealed to Margaret Mary "the infinitude of His love, at the same time, in the manner of a mourner." The Savior said,

> *Behold this Heart which has loved men so much and has loaded them with all benefits, and for this boundless love has had no return but neglect and contumely, and this often from those who were bound by a debt and duty of a more special love.*

Among the ways to make reparation to the Heart of Christ, the Pope urged the faithful to "make expiatory supplications and prayers, prolonged for a whole hour which is rightly called the Holy Hour" (*Miserentissimus Redemptor*, May 8, 1928). It was understood that the Holy Hour was to be made even as the original message was received by St. Margaret Mary, before the Holy Eucharist.

Pope Pius XII. With Pius XI's successor, we begin a new stage in the Church's teaching on the efficacy of prayer addressed to Christ really present in the Sacrament of the altar.

A year before his election to the See of Peter, Cardinal Pacelli was sent as papal legate to the International Eucharistic Congress at Budapest in Hungary. It was 1938, a year before the outbreak of the Second World War. The theme of Pacelli's address at the Congress was that Christ had indeed left this earth in visible form at His Ascension. But He is emphatically still on earth, the Jesus of history, in the Sacrament of His love.

Pius XII published forty-one encyclicals during his almost twenty year pontificate. One feature of these documents is their reflection of the doctrinal development that has taken place in the Catholic Church in modern times. Thus, development:

- In the Church's understanding of herself as the Mystical Body of Christ (*Mystici Corporis Christi*, 1943);

- In her understanding of the Bible (*Divino Afflante Spiritu*, 1943);

- In her understanding of the Blessed Virgin (*Deiparae Virginis Mariae*, 1946), proposing the definition of Mary's bodily Assumption into heaven.

The Encyclical *Mediator Dei* (1947) was on the Sacred Liturgy. As later events were to show, it became the doctrinal blueprint for the Constitution of the Liturgy of the Second Vatican Council.

Nine complete sections of *Mediator Dei* deal with "Adoration of the Eucharist." This provides the most authoritative explanation of what the Pope describes as "the worship of the Eucharist," which "gradually developed as something distinct from the Sacrifice of the Mass."

It seems best briefly to quote from these sections and offer some commentary.

1. Adoration of the Eucharist. The basis for all Eucharistic devotion is the fact that Christ in the Blessed Sacrament is the Son of God in human form.

The Eucharistic Food contains, as all are aware, "truly, really and substantially the Body and Blood together with the Soul and Divinity of Our Lord Jesus Christ." It is no wonder, then, that the Church, even from the beginning, adored the Body of Christ under the appearance of bread; this is evident from the very rites of the august Sacrifice, which prescribe that the sacred ministers should adore the Most Holy Sacrament by genuflecting or by profoundly bowing their heads.

The Sacred Councils teach that it is the Church's tradition right from the beginning, to worship "with the same adoration the Word Incarnate as well as His own flesh," and St. Augustine asserts that:

> *"No one eats that flesh without first adoring it," while he adds that "not only do we not commit a sin by adoring it, but we do sin by not adoring it" (Mediator Dei, paragraph 129-130).*

Everything else depends on this primary article of faith: that the Eucharist contains the living Christ, in the fullness of His human nature, and therefore really present under the sacred species; and in the fullness of His divine nature, and therefore to be adored as God.

2. Dogmatic Progress. There has been a deeper grasp by the Church of every aspect of the mystery of the Eucharist. But one that merits special attention is the growing realization, not only of Christ's sacrificial oblation in the Mass, but of His grace-filled presence outside of Mass.

> *It is on this doctrinal basis that the worship of adoring the Eucharist was founded and gradually developed as something distinct from the Sacrifice of the Mass. The reservation of the Sacred Species for the sick and those in danger introduced the praiseworthy custom of adoring the Blessed Sacrament which is reserved in our churches. This practice of adoration, in fact, is based on strong and solid reasons. For the Eucharist is at once a Sacrifice and a Sacrament: but it differs from the other Sacraments in this that it not only produces grace, but contains, in a permanent manner, the Author of grace Himself. When, therefore, the Church bids us adore Christ hidden behind the Eucharistic veils and pray to Him for the spiritual and temporal favors of which we ever stand in need, she manifests living faith in her divine Spouse who is present beneath these veils, she professes her gratitude to Him and she enjoys the intimacy of His friendship (131).*

The key to seeing why there should be a Eucharistic worship distinct from the Mass is that the Eucharist is Jesus Christ. No less than His contemporaries in Palestine adored and implored Him for the favors they needed, so we should praise and thank Him, and implore Him for what we need.

3. Devotional Development. As a consequence of this valid progress in doctrine, the Church has developed a variety of Eucharistic devotions.

Now, the Church in the course of centuries has introduced various forms of this worship which are ever increasing in beauty and helpfulness, as, for example, visits of devotion to the tabernacle, even every day, Benediction of the Blessed Sacrament; solemn processions, especially at the time of Eucharistic Congresses, which pass through cities and villages; and adoration of the Blessed Sacrament publicly exposed. Sometimes these public acts of adoration are of short duration. Sometimes they last for one, several and even for forty hours. In certain places they continue in turn in different churches throughout the year, while elsewhere adoration is perpetual, day and night (132).

To be stressed is that these are not merely passing devotional practices. They are founded on divinely revealed truth. And, as the Pope is at pains to point out, "these exercises of piety have brought a wonderful increase in faith and supernatural life to the Church militant upon earth."

Are these practices liturgical? "They spring from the inspiration of the Liturgy," answers Pius XII:

If they are performed with due decorum and with faith and piety, as the liturgical rules of the Church require, they are undoubtedly of the very greatest assistance in living the life of the Liturgy.

Does this not confuse the "Historic Christ" with the Eucharistic Christ? Not at all, says the Pope.

On the contrary, it can be claimed that by this devotion the faithful bear witness to and solemnly avow the faith of the Church that the Word of God is identical with the Son of the Virgin Mary, who suffered on the Cross, who is present in a hidden manner in the Eucharist and who reigns upon His heavenly throne. Thus St. John Chrysostom states: "When you see It (the Body of Christ) exposed, say to yourself — thanks to this Body, I am no longer dust and ashes, I am no more a captive but a freeman: hence I hope to obtain heaven and the good things that are there in store for me, eternal life, the heritage of the Angels, companionship with Christ" (134).

Among other forms of Eucharistic devotion recommended by Pope Pius XII, he gave special attention to Benediction of the Blessed Sacrament. He spoke of the:

great benefit in that custom which makes the priest raise aloft the Bread of Angels before congregations with heads bowed down in adoration and forming with It the sign of the cross."

This "implores the Heavenly Father to deign to look upon His Son who for love of us was nailed to the Cross and for His sake and through Him willed . . .to shower down heavenly favors upon those whom the Immaculate Blood of the Lamb has redeemed (135).

Pope John XXIII. Unlike his predecessor, John XXIII did not publish any extensive documentation on the Eucharistic Liturgy. But he took every occasion to urge the faithful, especially priests, to pray before the Blessed Sacrament.

In the life of a priest nothing could replace the silent and prolonged prayer before the altar. The adoration of Jesus, our God; thanksgiving, reparation for our sins and for those of all men, the prayer for so many intentions entrusted to Him, combine to raise that priest to a greater love for the Divine Master to whom he has promised faithfulness and for men who depend on his priestly ministry.

With the practice of this enlightened and fervent worship of the Eucharist, the spiritual life of the priest increases and there are prepared the missionary energies of the most valuable apostles.

All the while that he was urging priests to pray before the altar, the Pope reminded them that "the Eucharistic Prayer in the full sense is the Holy Sacrifice of the Mass" (Encyclical *Sacerdotii Nostri Primordia*, August 11, 1959). After all, without the Mass there would be no Real Presence. We might say that Christ's abiding presence in the Holy Eucharist is an extension of the Eucharistic sacrifice.

On the eve of the Second Vatican Council, Pope John participated in the Corpus Christi procession of the Blessed Sacrament in Rome. On that occasion, he composed an earnest prayer for Christ's blessings on the forthcoming council.

0 Jesus, look upon us from your Sacrament like the Good Shepherd, by which name the Angelic Doctor invokes you, and with him Holy Church. 0 Jesus, Good Shepherd, this is your flock, the flock that you have gathered from the ends of the earth, the flock that listens to your word of life, and intends to guard it, practice it and preach it. This is the flock that follows you meekly, 0 Jesus, and wishes so ardently to see, in the Ecumenical Council, the reflection of your loving face in the features of your Church, the Mother of all, the Mother who opens her arms and heart to all, and here awaits, trembling and trustful, the arrival of all her bishops (June 21, 1962).

Words could not be plainer. They could also not be more authoritative. The Vicar of Christ was teaching, by example, how effective prayer to our Lord in the Eucharist can be not only for ourselves personally, but for the whole Church of God.

Pope Paul VI. Although Pope John XXIII opened the Second Vatican Council and lived through its first session in 1962, he did not promulgate any of its sixteen documents. That was done by his successor, Pope Paul VI.

The first conciliar document issued by Paul VI was the Constitution on the Sacred Liturgy (December 4, 1963). Less than two years later, just before the last session of the council, he published the encyclical *Mysterium Fidei* (September 3, 1965). It is a remarkable document in several ways.

- It was issued during the Second Vatican Council.

- It opens with a glowing tribute to the Council's Constitution on the Liturgy.

- It praises those who "seek to investigate more profoundly and to understand more fruitfully the doctrine on the Holy Eucharist."

- But then it goes on to give "reasons for serious pastoral concern and anxiety." Specifically, Paul VI says that opinions are being spread which reinterpret "doctrine already defined by the Church," and in particular "the dogma of transubstantiation." (I)

Most of the encyclical, therefore, is a doctrinal analysis of the Real Presence. By all accounts, it is the most extensive and penetrating declaration in papal history on two articles of the Catholic faith: the corporeal presence of Jesus Christ in the Blessed Sacrament and His communication of grace through this Eucharistic presence now on earth.

1. The Real Presence. If we are to understand the sacramental presence of Christ in the Eucharist, "which constitutes the greatest miracle of its kind, we must listen with docility to the voice of the teaching and praying Church." What does the doctrine and devotion of the Church tell us?

This voice, which constantly echoes the voice of Christ, assures us that the way Christ is made present in this Sacrament is none other than by the change of the whole substance of the bread into His Body, and of the whole substance of the wine into His Blood, and that this unique and truly wonderful change the Catholic Church rightly calls transubstantiation. As a result of transubstantiation, the species of bread and wine undoubtedly take on a new meaning and a new finality, for they no longer remain ordinary bread and ordinary wine, but become the sign of something sacred, the sign of a spiritual food. However, the reason they take on this new significance and this new finality is simply because they contain a new reality which we may justly term ontological. There is no longer under the species what had been there before. It is something entirely different. Why? Not only because of the faith of the Church, but in objective reality. After the change of the substance or nature of the bread and wine into the Body and Blood of Christ, nothing remains of the bread and wine but the appearances, under which Christ, whole and entire, in His physical reality is bodily present (V).

Of course this presence is beyond our comprehension. Of course it is different from the way bodies are naturally present and therefore can be sensibly perceived. Subjectively, we cannot see or touch the Body of Christ in the Eucharist. But objectively (in reality) and ontologically (in His being) He is there.

2. Communication of Grace. Once the Real Presence is properly recognized, it is only logical to conclude that we should worship the Savior in the Blessed Sacrament. It is equally logical to expect Him to confer blessings on a sinful world by His presence among us. Three passages in *Mysterium Fidei* make this conclusion perfectly clear.

In the first statement, Pope Paul recalls the teaching of St. Cyril of Alexandria (died 444) who had been so active in defending the physical union of Christ's humanity in the Incarnation as well as in the Eucharist. The reason is that the Eucharist is the Incarnate Son of God who became, and remains, the Son of Mary.

St. Cyril of Alexandria rejects as folly the opinion of those who maintained that if a part of the Eucharist was left over for the following day, it did not confer sanctification. "For" he says, "neither Christ is altered nor His Holy Body changed, but the force and power and revivifying grace remain with it" (VI).

Once the elements of bread and wine have been consecrated and transubstantiation has taken place, the living Christ remains as long as the Eucharistic species remain. Then, because Christ is present, His humanity remains a source of life-giving grace.

In his second statement on the Eucharist as a channel of grace, Pope Paul carefully distinguishes between the Eucharist as Sacrifice and Communion, and the Eucharist as Presence.

> *Not only while the Sacrifice is offered and the Sacrament is received, but as long as the Eucharist is kept in our churches and oratories, Christ is truly the Emmanuel, that is "God with us." Day and night He is in our midst, He dwells with us, full of grace and truth. He restores morality, nourishes virtues, consoles the afflicted and strengthens the weak (VI).*

These verbs: *restores, nourishes, consoles* and *strengthens,* are all forms of divine grace which Christ confers by His presence in the Eucharist.

In his third statement on the efficacy of the Real Presence, Paul VI adds the final touch to his teaching. No doubt the living Savior in the Blessed Sacrament is there "full of grace and truth." But there must be a responsive faith on our part.

> *Anyone who approaches this August Sacrament with special devotion, and endeavors to return generous love for Christ's own infinite love, will experience and fully understand, not without spiritual joy and fruit, how precious is the life hidden with Christ in God, and how great is the value of converse with Christ. For there is nothing more consoling on earth, nothing more efficacious for advancing along the road of holiness (VI).*

The important word in that last sentence is "efficacious." Provided we approach the Real Presence with believing love, Christ will perform wonders of His grace in our lives.

Pope John Paul II. Building on the teaching of his predecessors, John Paul II has come to be known as the Pope of the Real Presence. In one document and address after another, he has repeated what needs repetition for the sake of emphasis:

> *The Eucharist, in the Mass and outside of the Mass, is the Body and Blood of Jesus Christ, and is therefore deserving of the worship that is given to the living God, and to Him alone (Opening address in Ireland, Phoenix Park, September 29, 1979).*

But the Pope has done more than merely repeat what had been said before. He placed the capstone on the Eucharistic teaching of the magisterium that we have been examining. He did so by explaining in the most unambiguous language that there is only one Sacrament of the Eucharist. Yet this one Sacrament confers grace in three different ways. Each manner of giving grace corresponds to the three forms in which the Eucharist has been instituted by Christ.

> *It is at one and the same time a Sacrifice-Sacrament, a Communion-Sacrament, and a Presence-Sacrament (Encyclical Redemptor Hominis, March 4, 1979, IV, 20).*

The revealed foundation for this conclusion is the fact of Christ's abiding presence in the Eucharist. It is the "Redeemer of Man" who by His Passion and death on the Cross merited the grace of our salvation. But it is mainly through the Eucharist that the same Jesus Christ now channels this grace to a sinful human race.

It is in this comprehensive sense that we can say, "the Church lives by the Eucharist, by the fullness of this Sacrament." This fullness, however, spans all three levels of its sacramental existence, where, by "sacrament" the Church means a sensible sign, instituted by Christ, through which invisible grace and inward sanctification are communicated to the soul.

The Mass is the Sacrifice-Sacrament of the Eucharist. As the Council of Trent declared, the Sacrifice of the Mass is not only an offering of praise and thanksgiving. It is also a source of grace:

> *By this oblation, the Lord is appeased. He grants grace and the gift of repentance, and He pardons wrongdoings and sins. The blessings of Redemption which Christ won for us by His bloody death on Calvary are now received in abundance through this unbloody oblation (September 17, 1562).*

Holy Communion is the Communion-Sacrament of the Eucharist. As the same Council of Trent defined, Christ present in the Eucharist is not only spiritually eaten, but also really and sacramentally. We actually receive His Body and Blood, and we are truly nourished by His grace. It was Christ's will "that this Sacrament be received as the soul's spiritual food, to sustain and build up those who live with His life." It is also to be "a remedy to free us from our daily defects and to keep us from mortal sin" (October 11, 1551).

The Real Presence is the Presence-Sacrament of the Eucharist. How? The Real Presence is a sacrament in every way that the humanity of Christ is a channel of grace to those who believe that the Son of God became man for our salvation.

Grace through the Humanity of Christ

The underlying theme of the Church's Eucharistic teaching is the fact of

Christ's consoling presence in the Blessed Sacrament. His Real Presence in the fullest sense; the substantial presence by which the whole and complete Christ, God and man, is present (Pope John Paul II, September 29,1979).

Once this fact of faith is recognized, it is not difficult to see why prayer before the Blessed Sacrament is so efficacious. Indeed it explains why, without a second thought, Catholics have simply referred to the Real Presence as the Blessed Sacrament. It is a sacrament, or better, it is the one sacrament which not only confers grace but contains the very source of grace, namely Jesus Christ.

As we read the Gospels, we are struck by the marvelous power that Christ's humanity had in effecting changes in the persons who came into contact with Him. Already in the womb of His mother, He sanctified the unborn John the Baptist the moment Elizabeth heard the voice of Mary. At Cana in Galilee, at His Mother's request, Jesus told the servants, "Fill the jars with water." When the steward tasted the water, it had turned into wine.

Jesus spoke with human lips when He preached the Sermon on the Mount, when He taught the parables, when he forgave sinners, when he rebuked the Pharisees, when He foretold His Passion and told His followers to carry the cross. Jesus touched the blind with human hands, and healed the lepers by speaking with a human voice. On one occasion a sick woman touched the hem of

31

His garment. "Immediately," relates St. Mark, "aware that power had gone out from Him, Jesus turned round in the crowd and said, 'who touched my clothes?'" The woman was instantly healed. Significantly, Jesus told her, "your faith has restored you to health."

All through His public ministry, the humanity of Christ was the means by which He enlightened the minds of His listeners, restored their souls to divine friendship, cured their bodies of disability and disease, and assured them of God's lasting peace. That is what St. John meant when, in the prologue of his Gospel, he said, "though the Law was given through Moses, grace and truth come through Jesus Christ." Why? Because Christ is the only-begotten Son of God who became flesh, and not only lived among us, but continues to live among us in the Eucharist.

In order to draw on these resources of infinite wisdom and power, available in the Eucharist, we must believe. In the words of the *Adoro Te*, we can say:

> *I believe everything that the Son of God has said, and nothing can be truer than this word of the Truth. Only the Godhead was hidden on the cross, but here the humanity is hidden as well. Yet I believe and acknowledge them both.*

Those who can thus speak to Christ in the Eucharist will learn from experience what the Church means when she tells us that the Real Presence is a sacrament. It is the same Savior who assumed our human nature to die for us on Calvary and who now dispenses through that same humanity, now glorified, the blessings of salvation.